DOG SEES GOD:
CONFESSIONS OF A
TEENAGE BLOCKHEAD

BY **BERT V. ROYAL**

★

★

DRAMATISTS
PLAY SERVICE
INC.

DOG SEES GOD: CONFESSIONS OF A TEENAGE BLOCKHEAD
Copyright © 2006, Bert V. Royal

All Rights Reserved

DOG SEES GOD was first presented by
Sorrel Tomlinson / File 14 Productions
at The 2004 New York International Fringe Festival,
a production of The Present Company.

Originally produced Off-Broadway,
in a limited engagement, by Sorrel Tomlinson.

Subsequently produced Off-Broadway
by Dede Harris and Martian Entertainment
in association with
Sharon Karmazin, Michelle Schneider, Mort Swinsky.

In addition, the following must appear on the title page of all programs distributed in connection with performances of the Play and in all instances in which the title of the Play appears for purposes of advertising, publicizing or otherwise exploiting the Play and/or a production thereof in size of type not less than 25% of the size of the largest, most prominent letter used for the title of the Play:

DOG SEES GOD has not been authorized or approved
in any manner by the Charles M. Schulz Estate or United Features Syndicate,
which have no responsibility for its content.

SPECIAL NOTE ON SONGS AND RECORDINGS
For performances of copyrighted songs, arrangements or recordings mentioned in this Play, the permission of the copyright owner(s) must be obtained. Other songs, arrangements or recordings may be substituted provided permission from the copyright owner(s) of such songs, arrangements or recordings is obtained; or songs, arrangements or recordings in the public domain may be substituted.

DOG SEES GOD was first presented as a reading on May 3, 2004, at the Barrow Street Theatre. It was directed by Anthony Barrile and produced by Sorrel Tomlinson. The cast was as follows:

CB .... Alexander Chaplin
CB'S SISTER .... Karen DiConcetto
VAN .... Daniel Franzese
MATT .... Marcus Chait
BEETHOVEN .... Daniel Letterle
TRICIA .... Mary Catherine Garrison
MARCY .... Melissa Picarello
VAN'S SISTER .... Jennifer Esposito

DOG SEES GOD had its World Premiere at the 2004 New York International Fringe Festival. It was presented at the SoHo Playhouse. It was directed by Susan W. Lovell and produced by Sorrel Tomlinson/File 14 Productions. The cast was as follows:

CB .... Michael Gladis
CB'S SISTER .... Karen DiConcetto
VAN .... Tate Ellington
MATT .... Jay Sullivan
BEETHOVEN .... Benjamin Schrader
TRICIA .... Bridget Barkan
MARCY .... Stelianie Tekmitchov
VAN'S SISTER .... Melissa Picarello
Understudies: Clay Black, Andrew Fleischer

DOG SEES GOD was extended for two weeks and Daniel Franzese assumed the role of Van.

DOG SEES GOD had another reading on May 9, 2005, at the Westside Theater. It was directed by Trip Cullman and produced by DeDe Harris and Sorrel Tomlinson. The cast was as follows:

CB .... Patrick Fugit
CB'S SISTER .... Alison Pill
VAN .... John Gallagher Jr.
MATT .... Mark Webber
BEETHOVEN .... Logan Marshall Green
TRICIA .... Michelle Trachtenberg
MARCY .... Anna Paquin
VAN'S SISTER .... Carly Jibson

DOG SEES GOD received its Off-Broadway premiere by Martian Entertainment and Dede Harris at the Century Center for the Performing Arts, opening on December 15, 2005. It was directed by Trip Cullman; the set design was by David Korins; the costume design was by Jenny Mannis; the lighting design was by Brian MacDevitt; the sound design was by Darron L. West; the general manager was Roy Gabay; the production stage manager was Lori Ann Zepp; the assistant stage manager was Tammy Scozzafava; and the production manager was Randall Etheredge. The cast was as follows:

CB .... Eddie Kaye Thomas
CB'S SISTER .... America Ferrara
VAN .... Keith Nobbs
MATT .... Ian Somerhalder
BEETHOVEN .... Logan Marshall-Green
MARCY .... Ari Graynor
TRICIA .... Kelli Garner
VAN'S SISTER .... Eliza Dushku
Understudies: Karen DiConcetto, Colby Chambers, Melissa Picarello

CHARACTERS

CB

CB'S SISTER

VAN

MATT

BEETHOVEN

MARCY

TRICIA

VAN'S SISTER

DOG SEES GOD:
CONFESSIONS OF A
TEENAGE BLOCKHEAD

"DEAR PEN PAL"

Lights up on a handsome, however currently sullen, teenager. His name is CB.

CB. Dear Pen Pal. I know it's been a few years since I last wrote you. I hope you're still there. I'm not sure you ever were. I never got any letters back from you when I was a kid. But in a way it was always very therapeutic. Everyone else judges everything I say. And here you are: some anonymous person who never says "boo." Maybe you just read my letters and laughed or maybe you didn't read my letters or maybe you don't even exist. It was pretty frustrating when I was young, but now I'm glad that you won't respond. Just listen. That's what I want. *(Beat.)* My dog died. I don't know if you remember, but I had a beagle. He was a good dog. My best friend. I'd had him as far back as I could remember, but one day last month, I went out to feed him and he didn't come bounding out of his red doghouse like usual. I called his name. But no response. I knelt down and called out his name. Still nothing. I looked in the doghouse. There was blood everywhere. Cowering in the corner was my dog. His eyes were wild and there was an excessive amount of saliva coming out of his mouth. He was unrecognizable. Both frightened and frightening at the same time. The blood belonged to a little yellow bird that had always been around. My dog and the bird used to play together. In a strange way, it was almost like they were best friends. I know that sounds stupid, but … Anyway, the bird had been mangled. Ripped apart. By my dog. When he saw that I could see what he'd done, his face changed to sadness and he let out a sound that felt like the word "help." I reached my hand into his doghouse. I know it was a dumb thing to do, but he looked like he needed me. His jaws snapped. I jerked my hand away before he could bite me. My parents called a center and they came and took him away. Later that day, they put him to sleep. They gave me his corpse in a cardboard box. When my dog died, that was when the rain cloud came back and everything went to hell … *(CB's sister enters wearing what can only be described as a black wedding dress. CB begins erecting a wooden cross on a mound of dirt in front of him. She joins him.)*

"CANIS EXEQUIAE"

CB and his sister are standing beside each other and staring at the wooden cross. A long silence passes. She takes a box of cigarettes out of her purse (that is shaped like a coffin) and offers one to him.

CB. Mom will kill you if she sees you smoking.
CB'S SISTER. *(Lighting the cigarette.)* Well, when she does, I hope you'll have the decency to bury me in an actual cemetery rather than the backyard. *(Another long silence passes.)* Do you think we should say a prayer or something?
CB. I guess.
CB'S SISTER. Okay. You can say it.
CB. I don't want to.
CB'S SISTER. Well, neither do I!
CB. I don't know what to say.
CB'S SISTER. Oh, stop being so melodramatic, Charles. No one's asking for a eulogy. Just a simple prayer. Ask the Earth to watch over him. Or something.
CB. He's dead. There's not a whole lot of that necessary.
CB'S SISTER. You're so morbid. What about his next life? I think we should pray to Hecate and ask her to make him a human. Someone we meet and become friends with.
CB. What???
CB'S SISTER. Hecate is the goddess of death. She's also a goddess

8

of reincarnation. It's Wiccan.

CB. Oh, so you're Wiccan this week? Glad that's cleared up. I can't keep your personalities straight! Last week, you go with a friend to a Baptist church, come home and proceed to tell Mom, Dad and me that we're going to hell because we watch TV. A mere NINE DAYS LATER, you're Elvira, Mistress of the Dark. We can't keep up with you! FIND. AN. IDENTITY.

CB'S SISTER. You're one to talk!

CB. What could you possibly mean by that?! I'm always the same!

CB'S SISTER. *(Venomously.)* That's nothing to brag about. *(Beat.)* Just drop it, okay? You don't tell me how to live my life and I won't tell you how to live yours. *(Silence.)*

CB. I thought there'd be a bigger turnout. *(She gives him a funny look.)* Well, he was popular. All our friends loved him. I just thought people would actually show up to pay their respects.

CB'S SISTER. You invited our friends?

CB. A few.

CB'S SISTER. You are so embarrassing!

CB. You're dressed like the bride of Frankenstein and I'm embarrassing?

CB'S SISTER. Shut up about my dress!

CB. *(Sotto voce; to self.)* This is not the way he would've wanted his funeral.

CB'S SISTER. He was a DOG, Charles. They shit on the ground and lick themselves. Ceremony is probably not key here. He was just a fucking dog.

CB. Oh yeah? Well, he was MY fucking dog. So, fuck you.

CB'S SISTER. He was my fucking dog, too! So, fuck you! *(Beat.)*

CB. He never liked you.

CB'S SISTER. I suppose he told you this.

CB. He didn't have to. It was apparent. He barely tolerated you.

CB'S SISTER. I hate you.

CB. Big loss.

CB'S SISTER. You're a dickhead, CB.

CB. *(Exploding.)* JUST SAY YOUR FUCKING PRAYER! *(Long pause.)*

CB'S SISTER. He was your fucking dog. You fucking say it. *(She storms off.)*

"NIRVANA"

CB and Van sit on the sad remnant of a brick wall. Van is smoking a joint. He offers it to CB.

VAN. You wanna hit this?

CB. No. Thanks.

VAN. *(Smiling.)* It's kind bud. You sure, man?

CB. Nah, I'm good.

VAN. I've been meaning to tell you — I'm sorry about your dog.

CB. Thanks, man.

VAN. He was a good dog.

CB. Yeah. He was.

VAN. But he was old. It was long past his time. Still — he was a good dog. I totally wanted to come to your funeral party thingy, but I was waiting on a delivery from the Doober.

CB. What do you think happens when we die?

VAN. Do you mean, like, do I believe in heaven?

CB. Yeah.

VAN. Nah, man. I'm a Buddhist.

CB. Since when?

VAN. It's kind of a new development.

CB. Well, what do Buddhists believe happens when you die?

VAN. Buddha believed that one of two things happens. Either you are reborn or you dissolve into nothingness. Oddly enough, the former is punishment and the latter, reward. We Buddhists believe that the corporeal body is the source of all suffering and a liberation from the body into nothingness, or nirvana, is the fuckin' way to go.

CB. Don't you find that depressing?

VAN. Liberation?

CB. Nothingness.

VAN. I think I'd kind of like to be nothingness. Because even nothing is something, right? *(He shows his hand to CB.)* What am I holding in my hand?

CB. Nothing.

VAN. One would say that, yes. But in that nothingness is a thousand things, right? Particles and atoms and tens of thousands of

10

things that we might not even know about yet. I could be holding in my hand the secrets of the universe and the answers to everything.

CB. You're stoned.

VAN. Damn straight. *(CB laughs.)* Why this interest in the afterlife? Is this about your dog?

CB. Just curious.

VAN. Dude, we all have to let go of things from our childhood. Do you remember when you and my sister burned my blanket to teach me that?

CB. Yeah. It was only two months ago. If I'd known that it would lead to her being — well — I wouldn't have let her do it.

VAN. I was so pissed at you guys.

CB. The thing was fuckin' nasty, man.

VAN. *(Pissed.)* Still. Y'all suck.

CB. I think you were about to make a point.

VAN. I was?

CB. Never mind. I think I got it.

VAN. My point is, Chuck B., that life — it does go on. Even without the things that have been there since the beginning. The things that we think define us, don't mean shit in the grand scheme of things. Us defines us. Not things or other people or pets. Like, me without my blanket — it's still me. I miss my fuckin' blanket, though. That was a dick thing y'all did.

CB. Three words for you, bro — *(One finger.)* Pubic. *(Two fingers.)* Lice. *(Three fingers.)* Infestation.

VAN. Could've been fixed.

CB. Hey, we let you keep the ashes.

VAN. I smoked 'em.

CB. You what?

VAN. I rolled 'em with some good herb and smoked that shit up.

CB. That's sick.

VAN. Now, my blanket and I are like one forever.

CB. That's seriously disturbed, dawg.

VAN. We all handle grief in different ways.

CB. Can't be good for you.

VAN. Dude! Showed you two! Tryin' to mess with my shit. HA!

CB. Hey, how is your sister doing?

VAN. She's good. The doctors say that she's getting better. *(Beat.)* Damn, I miss that bitch.

CB. So do I.

VAN. This conversation is a major downer, amigo. Dead dogs, missing sisters, burning blankets. Let's talk about something happy.
CB. Like what? *(They sit in silence. The lights fade slowly out.)*

"WHERE SWINE LIVE"

A piercingly loud school bell rings. Welcome to Thursday morning. CB stands center stage wearing his backpack. Matt enters. He is extremely attractive and just as obnoxious.

MATT. CB, my nigga! What is UP, dawg?
CB. N'much, man. *(They punch each other's fists.)*
MATT. Are we going to this party on Saturday?
CB. Where?
MATT. Marcy's parents are out of town. Plen-TAY of virgini-TAY. *(He thinks this rhymes.)* Hey, I think Marcy's all into you. Maybe it's time you're all "into her." Y'know't I'm sayin'? *(He humps the air. And then gets serious.)* Oh, hey man. I'm sorry about your dog. That's rough.
CB. Yeah. Thanks.
MATT. You could prob'ly use that to get some pussy, though. Bitches are suckers for that shit. Best sex I ever had was when I told this girl that my mom kicked it. She "consoled" me for four hours straight! If you can whip up a few fake tears, it'll definitely help the cause. Watch and learn. *(Feigning sadness.)* "Life has no meaning! Why couldn't it've been me?" *(Slipping to sexual.)* "Oh yeah, baby. I'm almost there. That's good. That's real good. Mom would've wanted it this way." I'm tellin' you. Works like a charm. Plus, girls are suckers for animals. A dead dog, that's NICE.
CB. Hey man, what do you think happens when you die?
MATT. Well, that's a good question, CB. I'm glad you asked. It's something I've thought about many times. And the way I see it is: Okay, when you start life you're coming out of this gigantic vagina that's bigger than you are. Right?
CB. Right.
MATT. *(Smiling slyly.)* Well, I think when we die we're goin' back in. *(Thinking about this.)* Except this time, it's not our mom's.

CB. Right. *(He pulls out a bag of coke and does a bump.)*

MATT. You want?

CB. No. Thanks. *(He shoves the bag back into his pocket.)*

MATT. *(Singing operatically, to the tune of Handel's "Hallelujah Chorus.")* I LOVE PUSSY! I love pussy! Pussy! Pussy! *(Beethoven enters walking across the stage, carrying schoolbooks. He rolls his eyes at Matt as he passes.)* Speaking of pussy ... *(To Beethoven.)* What the fuck are you looking at, cocksucker? *(To CB.)* Did you see the way that fuckin' faggot just looked at me? *(Shouting to Beethoven as he exits.)* You fuckin' fairy, I'll kick your fuckin' ass. I fuckin' hate that kid! *(CB's sister charges onstage and pushes Matt. This time, she's wearing "gangsta bitch" attire.)*

CB'S SISTER. Leave him alone! Why are you so mean to him?

MATT. *(Condescendingly.)* Aren't you missing the Barbie Tea Party?

CB'S SISTER. Why are you SUCH a DICK?!

MATT. What was that? You said you wanted to suck my dick?

CB'S SISTER. You are so gross.

MATT. CB, is it okay if your sister sucks my dick?

CB'S SISTER. *(To CB.)* I can't believe you let him talk to people like that.

CB. Fuck off, squirt. *(Matt mimes jerking off.)*

MATT. "Squirt" being the operative word here.

CB'S SISTER. You guys are disgusting. *(She starts to leave, but then turns around. A smile spreads across her face.)* Hey Matt. Question for you. Where do swine live? *(She runs offstage. Matt clenches his fists. Rage is coursing all through his body. CB puts a hand on his shoulder and he relaxes.)*

MATT. *(Through clenched teeth.)* You know how I feel about people calling me that.

CB. Ease up. She didn't say it. Deep breath. Let it go. *(He takes a deep breath and is okay.)*

MATT. Because she's YOUR sister and YOU'RE my best friend, I won't beat the shit out of her.

CB. And then there's that whole thing about her being a girl, too.

MATT. *(Realizing.)* Right.

CB. You do have a temper, dude.

MATT. And it all started with that little faggot. I fuckin' hate that kid. He's always looking at me like he's in love with me. I fucking hate that kid. *(They exit.)*

13

"THE PIANIST AND THE PLATYPUS"

*Beethoven walks across the stage, as before carrying his books.
CB's sister runs on after him.*

CB'S SISTER. Hey, Beethoven! Wait up!
BEETHOVEN. *(To himself.)* Oh God. *(Despite his trying to get
away, she catches up to him.)*
CB'S SISTER. Hey, don't let those guys get to you.
BEETHOVEN. I don't.
CB'S SISTER. They're just assholes.
BEETHOVEN. Okay.
CB'S SISTER. Where are you going?
BEETHOVEN. It's lunch period.
CB'S SISTER. Wanna sit together?
BEETHOVEN. I'm not going to the cafeteria.
CB'S SISTER. Where are you going?
BEETHOVEN. I've got … stuff to do.
CB'S SISTER. Are you coming to the drama club meeting after
school?
BEETHOVEN. I'm not in the drama club.
CB'S SISTER. You should be! It's really fun!
BEETHOVEN. Aren't you the only member?
CB'S SISTER. Well, yeah, but it's given me a lot of time to work
on my one-woman show. I'm thinking about calling it *Cocooning
into Platypus.* Do you like that title?
BEETHOVEN. *(Totally uninterested.)* Sure, why not?
CB'S SISTER. It's about a caterpillar who longs to evolve into a
platypus instead of a butterfly. It's sort of a metaphor for —
BEETHOVEN. I've gotta go. *(He starts to exit.)*
CB'S SISTER. Are you going to Marcy's party on Saturday?
BEETHOVEN. I'd rather gnaw off my left arm. *(He leaves. She
calls out after him.)*
CB'S SISTER. Maybe we could get together this weekend. I could
do your tarot cards or maybe we could go to a poetry reading or
something. *(No response.)* Bye! *(Lights out.)*

"SPORK"

Cafeteria. Lunchtime. Two girls, Tricia and Marcy, enter with their lunch trays and take a seat at an empty table.

TRICIA. So, he was all like, "Woh woh woh. Woh woh. Woh woh woh wowoh woh." He is such a dick! So, I'm like: "Excuse me, Mr. Von Pfefferkorn, but just because I can't define metaphor doesn't mean I don't know what one is, you stupid buttwad!"

MARCY. You called Mr. Von Pfefferkorn a buttwad?!

TRICIA. No, of course not. I added that to the story for dramatic effect.

MARCY. Oh.

TRICIA. I begged and pleaded to God not to put me in his class. I wanted to be in Mr. Griffin's lit class. He gives A's to anyone with tits. But, no, I get the fag.

MARCY. Do you really think Mr. Von Pfefferkorn is a fag?

TRICIA. Well, if he were straight, then obviously I wouldn't be failing his class.

MARCY. Totally!

TRICIA. The thing is: I really think that God is punishing me for sleeping with Fatty-fat Frieda's boyfriend.

MARCY. You slept with Craig Kovelsky?!

TRICIA. I blew him. You knew that! I totally told you right after it happened!

MARCY. You did not!!

TRICIA. I so did!

MARCY. Ewwwww!

TRICIA. I was drunk, okay? Speaking of, is anybody looking??

MARCY. No, sir.

TRICIA. *(Condescendingly.)* Sweetie, you've gotta stop calling me that. *(Over the following dialogue, Tricia reaches into her backpack and produces a large bottle of vodka. She pours a large amount into her milk carton, she passes it to Marcy, who does the same. Tricia quickly puts the bottle back into her backpack. Marcy produces a bottle of Kahlua from her backpack, and they repeat this action. They take their cartons, close them and shake vigorously, in unison. Switching gears:)*

I think I did it, subconsciously, just because I fucking hate Frieda Fatass.

MARCY. Oh my God! I know, right?!

TRICIA. Totally right! I mean, seriously, whenever one of us is upset over a real problem, she has to butt her fat ass in and start crying about how she can't stop puking up her food.

MARCY. It's soooo pathetic!

TRICIA. I swear to God, if I have to hear her bitch one more time about how Craig won't sleep with her until she loses weight, I'm going to stick my foot up her ass. That is, if I can find the entrance. If she's bulimic, will someone please tell me why she's such a heifer? I mean, come on, Frieda.

MARCY. She told me the other day she was on a diet and I was thinking, like: What? You can't eat anything larger than your head? Survey says —

MARCY and TRICIA. YOU'RE FAT!

MARCY. Take your finger out of your throat and drag your ass to Lane Bryant.

TRICIA. And speaking of her fashion sense, why is she always wearing that shirt that says WWJD? What the hell is that supposed to mean? Who wants jelly doughnuts? *(Marcy spits her drink all over the place.)*

MARCY. *(Laughing.)* I think it's: What would Jesus do.

TRICIA. Well, He wouldn't wear that ugly-ass shirt with those nasty-ass spandex shorts. SPANDEX! Who wears Spandex?!

MARCY. Somebody needs to explain "camel toe" to her.

TRICIA. Her body is so gross! *(Imitating Frieda.)* "I'm not just the president of the Itty Bitty Titty Commitee; I'm also a client!" Blecch! "What would Jesus do?"

MARCY. He wouldn't let Darryl Farmer finger Him under the bleachers during a pep rally, that's for damn sure!

TRICIA. Totally! Now, what should we drink to?

MARCY. How about "life, liberty and the pursuit of happiness"?

TRICIA. Marcy, I hate to tell you this. But sometimes you are really bland.

MARCY. Screw you! I am not.

TRICIA. Well, hello!!! There's a thousand things in this world to toast to and you pick the lamest one ever!

MARCY. Okay. Here's to … *(Looking down at her tray.)* Tater tots.

TRICIA. Well, that's slightly more interesting. *(They "clink" cartons and down their drinks.)*

MARCY. I'm buzzed.

TRICIA. Me too. *(They stare at their plates. Tricia picks up her spork and studies it.)* The spork is a great invention. Simple, but effective. It's like, who came up with it? *(Tricia makes them another round.)*

MARCY. The spork was invented in the 1940s. After the war, when the U.S. Army occupied Japan, General MacArthur decreed that the use of chopsticks was uncivilized, and the conquered should use forks and spoons like — quote — the civilized world. But fearing that the Japanese might rise up, revolt and retake their country with their forks, he and the U.S. Army invented the much less dangerous spork, which was then introduced into the public schools. But really all a spork is, is a plastic descendant of the runcible spoon. *(Tricia is shocked.)*

TRICIA. Okay. Umm. How did you know that?

MARCY. Can you keep a secret?

TRICIA. Can Frieda eat a moon pie in only two bites?

MARCY. No. Seriously. I'm the smartest person in the world.

TRICIA. Yeah. And she's the skinniest.

MARCY. No, it's true. I was part of this government experiment in elementary school. It was a drug that made kids, like, super geniuses. Able to retain everything they learned. But the drug had a side effect …

TRICIA. *(Without missing a beat.)* Backne?

MARCY. Shut up, bitch! You know I'm sensitive about that!

TRICIA. I am not sorry, girlfriend. Why don't you just go to the damn dermatologist?

MARCY. *(Annoyed.)* Can I please finish my story? So, this miracle super genius drug fucks with all the kids' hormones and turns everybody into, like, horny children. Like, all these third graders are running around humping, like, everything. *(Tricia is dumbfounded by this information.)*

TRICIA. That is so weird! You WERE really smart when we were kids! And really horny … *(Marcy bursts out laughing.)*

MARCY. Got you! Ha ha! You're so fucking gullible!

TRICIA. You're a snatch!

MARCY. You'll believe anything.

TRICIA. How did you know all that stuff about the spork?

MARCY. Duh! I looked it up on the Internet. Every time we do get drunk at school, you pick up a spork and say, "The spork is such a great invention. I wonder where it came from." So, I decided that I was going to be ready one day with the answer.

TRICIA. *(Sarcastically.)* How brilliant of you. *(There is a moment of silence. They both finish off their drinks. Tricia turns hers over and nothing comes out. She pulls the bottle of vodka out of her bag and pours a shitload of it into the empty milk carton. Marcy slides her carton over and Tricia refills hers, as well. They both begin to down the vodka.)* I'm depressed. *(They look at each other and break out into inebriated laughter. CB and Matt enter with trays and sit with them. Tricia and Marcy try to act normal.)*

CB. Hey.

MATT. What's up, sluts?

TRICIA. You wish.

MARCY. What's up?

CB. Nothing.

TRICIA. *(To CB.)* Sorry we couldn't make it to your dog's funeral.

CB. That's okay.

MARCY. But, don't you think it's kind of weird? Having a funeral for a dog?

CB. I guess. Whatever.

TRICIA. Well, he's in a better place.

MARCY. Want a drink?

CB. No thanks.

MATT. *(Realizing.)* Oh shit! You guys are wasted!

CB. What do you mean by "a better place"?

TRICIA. I don't know. Like doggy heaven or something? *(Marcy and Tricia laugh.)*

CB. Do you really believe that?

TRICIA. Hell no.

MARCY. Not a chance.

TRICIA. I was just saying it to be polite.

CB. You don't believe in heaven?

TRICIA. Well, yeah. For people. But dogs? I don't think so.

CB. So, what happens to them?

TRICIA and MARCY. Maggot food! *(Squealing at the jinx.)* I love you!

TRICIA. Sorry, but that's what we think.

MARCY. Dogs are gross.

TRICIA. If there are dogs in heaven, I want to go to hell.

MARCY. You're probably going there anyway, bitch!

TRICIA. Yay! We can carpool! *(They laugh again. CB realizes that this is an impossible conversation.)*

CB. *(Exiting.)* See you guys.

TRICIA. *(Flirtatiously.)* So, Matt, are you coming to Marcy's party? *(Matt takes out a bottle of hand sanitizer from his pocket and uses it.)*

MATT. I dunno. Gotta check my calendar.

TRICIA. You don't even know how to read.

MATT. *(Feigning retarded.)* Very funny, Tricia.

TRICIA. That's okay. I like 'em dumb.

MARCY. You should bring CB with you.

MATT. CB said he'd only go if you give him head and let him cum on your tits. *(The girls shriek.)*

TRICIA. You're a pig! *(Matt goes stiff, as before. He's pissed. Defensively:)* What? I didn't say it! *(He lets go of his anger and smiles. Marcy takes a handful of tater tots from his plate.)*

MATT. You can't touch my food like that!

MARCY. *(With her mouth full.)* Why not?

MATT. Aw man! Don't chew with your mouth open! That's disgusting! *(Regaining composure.)* Look. There are germs all over your hand, so when you put your hand in someone else's food, you contaminate that person's food. And when you chew with your mouth open, little pieces of gnashed food, mixed with your saliva in turn fly out of your mouth and onto other people's plates. It's gross. And now I can't eat this. *(He stands and exits. Marcy and Tricia are just staring after him.)*

TRICIA. I don't get it. This is the same kid who used to wallow in filth. A virtual cloud of dirt followed him everywhere he went and now he's like some germophobe. And the nickname thing! It's like who cares?

MARCY. He does.

TRICIA. I'm so gonna have sex with him at your party.

MARCY. Do you think CB will come?

TRICIA. On your tits, apparently. *(They giggle, look at their empty cartons and a longing sweeps over them.)*

MARCY. *(Slurring.)* We should revolt. We should rise up with our sporks in hand and protest against … against …

TRICIA. Fatty-fat-fat-fuckin'-fat-fat-fatty-fatass-fuckin' Frieda!

MARCY. And Mr. Von Pfefferkorn!

TRICIA. And … and … tater tots! Who the hell wants to eat these fucking things anyway?! *(She begins tossing tater tots all over the place.)*

MARCY. Yeah! *(They awkwardly and drunkenly climb atop the cafeteria table, chuckling. They hold their sporks high in the air. Van enters.)*

VAN. What are you two doing?
MARCY and TRICIA. We're revolting!!! *(They look at each other and once again start laughing. They fall off the table in hysterics. Lights out.)*

"A SEGUE I SUPPOSE"

Lights up on CB, who addresses the audience, continuing his letter.

CB. I heard a song. The song was simple. Much more simple than what he usually played. I was passing by the music room when I heard it. *(Beat.)* I don't know if Fredric Chopin had a dog, but maybe he did? And maybe he wrote that song because his dog died, too. *(Thinking about this.)* I don't know. Maybe. *(He gets lost in the song.)*

"THE VIPER'S NEST"

Lights up on Beethoven playing Chopin's "Prelude #4 in E Minor, Op. 28/4" on the piano. He has a black eye. CB enters unseen by Beethoven. He stands and listens to the music, as if hypnotized by it. He begins to cry silently, but then accidentally lets out a sob. Beethoven abruptly stops, spins around and sees him. CB pulls himself together.

BEETHOVEN. You're not supposed to be in here. I have permission to practice during lunch. But nobody else is supposed to be in here.
CB. You've gotten really good. I mean, you always were, but — Who wrote that? Beethoven?
BEETHOVEN. Chopin.
CB. Do you mind if I just listen for a little while? *(Beethoven resumes.)* God. This is really embarrassing. *(Pause.)* My dog died. He got rabies. They, um, had to put him under. I looked up rabies

20

on the Internet. It's an acute viral infection. It's transmitted through infected saliva. I guess he must have been bitten by something that had it. Maybe a fox or a raccoon. Bats can have it too. It travels from the bite to the spinal cord and the brain. Then the victim gets a really high fever and uncontrollable excitement, then spasms of the throat muscles. That's what causes them to salivate. They can't swallow water. Another word for the infection is "hydrophobia," which of course means "fear of water." Can you imagine not being able to swallow? That must suck. *(Beginning to ramble.)* It's weird. We had him vaccinated when he was a puppy. I guess it doesn't always work. *(Beat.)* We had a funeral for him. Well, my sister and me did. I think I was supposed to say something, but I couldn't think of anything to say. I just stood there, frozen, like an idiot. My brain went numb and that's never happened to me before. I mean, there's always something going on up there, right? Even in the subconscious. People meditate to clear their minds. I don't get that. I don't ever want to have a clear mind again. I guess I was thinking, by burying him, that I'd have some closure or feel his presence there or something and I didn't and that just freaked me out, so I don't know. I mean, have you ever had someone close to you die and you can't stop thinking about them and what's happened to them? It's like you're stuck in this morbid place and there's so much death that you feel like your head is going to explode and it makes you think that you're not even there. That maybe you're dead, too. *(Beethoven slams his fist down on the piano, making a cacophonous chord.)* What?

BEETHOVEN. Well, it's just that you haven't spoken to me in years. Except to call me a "faggot" or to dislocate my shoulder and all of a sudden I get a stream-of-consciousness monologue about your dead dog while I'm trying to spend the only moments of my day that don't truly SUCK. And, you see, there's some missing component to this conversation, other than an attentive listener. A segue, I suppose? Forgive my bluntness. Please don't hit me. But I could give two shits about you or your vacant mind or your morbid curiosities or your dead fucking dog, so why don't you just leave?

CB. I never dislocated your shoulder!

BEETHOVEN. According to my doctor, you did. In shop class last spring, you twisted my arm behind my back and told me that you wouldn't let go until I said that — and I quote — "I like to get it up the ass."

CB. I was just playing around with you.

BEETHOVEN. That makes me feel a lot better! At least I know it was all in good fun. Now I remember. Through my screaming and the searing pain, I definitely recall hearing laughter. Anyway I can contribute to the fun of the group …

CB. We were just messing with you.

BEETHOVEN. Fuck you, CB! I'd rather you say "we beat the shit out of you because we can't stand you" than to say you're just "messing" with me! That implies light teasing or slightly opprobrious behavior. I haven't had lunch in the cafeteria in two and a half years for fear of going home with some part of it smeared across my shirt! I haven't been in a bathroom on campus since the time my head got slammed into the wall. I believe you were there.

CB. I didn't do that!

BEETHOVEN. Yeah?! Well, you didn't stop it either! And the faculty doesn't care. You know what I'm so sick of hearing? "They only pick on you because of their own insecurities." The classic guidance counselor line! "Oh geez, Mrs. Blank, since you put it that way, my head doesn't hurt so much anymore!" And what really kills me is that everybody wonders why kids bring guns to school and shoot you fuckers down. Maybe you're not the bully, but you stand idly by and watch. In my eyes that makes you even worse. So — Please. Just. Go.

CB. Maybe if you didn't act so —

BEETHOVEN. What? What, CB? How do I act?

CB. Well. Gay.

BEETHOVEN. And how does one act gay? *(Silence.)* By playing the piano? Oh, it must be all those times I ogle the football team. Maybe I'll stop carrying around a pink purse. Or openly sucking dick in plain view of the entire student body! What?! What is it?!

CB. You're being hostile and I'm just trying to talk to you like a civilized —

BEETHOVEN. I don't want to talk to you!!! I just want to be left alone! I don't need social pointers. All I need from you is an apology for the five minutes that you've stolen from my day!

CB. See, this is why you don't have any friends.

BEETHOVEN. I think we both know why I don't have any friends.

CB. Oh, don't be so melodramatic!

BEETHOVEN. You're in here crying about a dead dog and I'M being melodramatic?!

CB. Just shut the fuck up about my dog, okay? *(Beethoven gets up*

in his face.)
BEETHOVEN. Or what? You'll hit me? Go ahead. I'll show you how people get hurt and don't run away to cry like a big fucking baby. *(Beethoven shoves CB. He's had it. CB doesn't fight back. Beethoven is hitting him as hard as he can but CB isn't budging. Beethoven relents and CB begins to laugh and his laugh is getting bigger and bigger.)* What's so funny, asshole?
CB. I'm sorry. Nothing.
BEETHOVEN. I don't see anything to laugh at.
CB. It's just that I was scared of you for, like, a second. *(Beethoven joins in on the laughter.)*
BEETHOVEN. I'm sorry.
CB. No, it's okay. I deserved it. *(Beat.)* Promise me you won't bring a gun to school.
BEETHOVEN. I don't know where to get one. *(A silence.)* You were one of my best friends. You all were. I just don't get it.
CB. It's no consolation, but — well, can I be honest?
BEETHOVEN. Yeah.
CB. No one knew what to say to you after your dad got arrested. It was awkward.
BEETHOVEN. It was more awkward for me.
CB. I'm sorry that we weren't there for you.
BEETHOVEN. That means a lot.
CB. See, now you're being sarcastic again.
BEETHOVEN. No, I wasn't.
CB. *(Laughing.)* It's hard to tell with you. *(Beethoven laughs as well. CB extends his hand.)* Truce?
BEETHOVEN. I wasn't fighting a war, but okay. Truce. *(He shakes his hand. Their hands are together for longer than expected. CB pulls his away.)*
CB. Are you — ?
BEETHOVEN. I don't know. I've never had sex, so it would be hard to say at this point.
CB. But what about — ?
BEETHOVEN. My dad? I don't think that's considered sex. *(A longer than average silence.)*
CB. Do you remember how my dog used to howl whenever you played the piano?
BEETHOVEN. Yeah. I always found it pretty insulting.
CB. He was singing along. What do you think happens to pets when they die?

BEETHOVEN. They go to heaven.

CB. You believe in heaven?

BEETHOVEN. Sure. There has to be some reward for having to live through this.

CB. And you think there are animals there? In heaven?

BEETHOVEN. "The wolf will live with the lamb, the leopard will lie down with the goat, and the calf and the lion and the yearling together; and a little child will lead them. The cow will feed with the bear, their young will lie down together, and the lion will eat straw like the ox. The infant will play near the hole of the cobra, and the young child put his hand into the viper's nest."

CB. But my dog killed a living thing. Wouldn't God be mad?

BEETHOVEN. He was sick, CB. He couldn't help it. *(Was he talking about his father? He looks at CB, who looks depressed.)* You know they say a dog sees God in his master. A cat looks in the mirror.

CB. *(Chuckling.)* I hate cats.

BEETHOVEN. Me too. *(CB stares at him for a long moment, then smiles. He stands up and walks over to the piano. He sits down and begins to play the bass part of a song like "Heart and Soul."* Beethoven stands and joins him at the piano to play the treble part — of course, stylistically. CB stops, prompting Beethoven to, as well. He looks at him again for a long moment. He grabs Beethoven and kisses him, long and passionately. He pulls away. CB stares at him, almost blankly, then he stands and exits, leaving Beethoven a little out of sorts. Lights out.)*

"DRAMA"

Lights up on CB's sister. She performs to the audience. The following can only be described as BAD.

CB'S SISTER. Metamorphosis. Transformation. Evolution. Change. Evolution. Change. Changing evolution. I am a teenage caterpillar. I know of these things. For soon, I'll spin a cocoon. And from the silklike craft that I will create, a magnificent creature will

* See Special Note on Songs and Recordings on copyright page.

emerge. No. Not a butterfly. For butterflies are a dime a dozen. Destined to flit about for a day or so, then drop dead. Or have its wings ripped off by a demented child. Or have its body pinned to a piece of cheap foam core and matted underneath a cheap frame and hung in the bathroom of an elderly woman who reeks of Preparation-H and Vicks VapoRub. *(Beat.)* This will not be my fate. This CANNOT be my fate. I will become a platypus. It's not impossible. It's just never been done before. It's only a matter of time, you see. If I stay in my cocoon longer, I'll change from a butterfly to a swallow and then from a swallow to a duck and then from a duck to a platypus. It's all just a matter of time. And time I have. I will wait to become a platypus. I will be an extraordinary creature. *(The lights fade as she pulls a silk scarf from her pocket and begins to wrap it around herself.)*

"YOU'RE INVITED!"

Lights up on Marcy. A vibrant tune plays under the following, indicating a party is about to happen. As Marcy delivers the following, the cast (with the exception of Beethoven) enters and positions themselves around the stage. As they get to their marks they stand like statues, scattered around the space.

MARCY.
> You're cordially invited to the party of the year.
> My folks went to Bali and left my ass here.
> So what better way to get my revenge,
> Than throwing a shindig that would make them both cringe?
> We'll have some kegs, so chip in some cash,
> Or else just bring from your parents' stash!
> I'm sure that someone will bring some grass,
> Remember the rule: puff, puff, pass!
> Anyone who plans on dropping E,
> Will have to bring a pill for me.
> And anyone up for a little "phys ed,"
> Well, you can use my parents' bed!
> So, Mommy and Daddy I'm sure will regret,

I'm throwing a party you'll never forget.

(A strange melody plays over the beat, prompting the gang to begin dancing bizarrely [as they did when they were younger]. The song explodes and so do they. They launch into a rousing dance. Marcy and Tricia are grinding against each other. Matt is grinding behind Tricia and CB is grinding behind Marcy.)

TRICIA. *(To Marcy.)* Oh. My. God. Did you see Frieda? Naturally curly hair, my naturally skinny ass!

MARCY. She's such a wannabe!

TRICIA. And a never-will-be!

MARCY and TRICIA. I hate her! *(They squeal because they said it in unison.)* I love you! *(They squeal again and grind harder.)*

MATT. Dude! Y'all should make out! For CB here. He's only got a week left to live. Let the guy die with a hard-on. *(They tease like they're going to do it.)*

TRICIA. Matt. You're so … dirty.

MARCY. If CB wants a hard-on, I'm sure I can take care of that, solo … *(Matt and CB slap hands over Tricia and Marcy. Squinting off:)* Is someone … Is someone defecating on the barbecue? Oh. My. God. *(Charging off the stage.)* You can't do that! That's disgusting! *(Van dances over to CB's sister, who is dancing freakishly by herself.)*

VAN. Hey, angel tits, wanna dance — horizontally?

CB'S SISTER. Fuck off, dick! I'm waiting for someone. *(She exits the stage. He continues dancing — breakdancing, in fact.)*

MARCY. *(Reentering, seething, to Van.)* Your retard little brother is cooking his feces on my parents' grill! *(She charges past to Tricia and drags her away from between CB and Matt.)*

MARCY. Did CB say anything about the prom?

TRICIA. In, like, the fourteen seconds you were gone? Sorry, hon.

MARCY. Tricia, just FIND OUT! Or I'll cut you. *(Looking offstage.)* Franklin, get that blunt away from Miss Kittywhiskers right this instant!

MATT. Oh, dude, bring it over here! *(Beethoven enters, carefully. He's holding a cup and sipping slowly. Matt spots him.)* What the fuck is HE doing here?!

ALL. *(To Beethoven; except CB.)* What the fuck are YOU doing here?! *(The music stops. Matt walks over to Beethoven and gets up in his face.)*

MATT. I think you must've missed the fine print at the bottom of the invitation that said: No queers. Sorry you came all this way, buddy, but you're going to have to turn around and follow the breadcrumbs back to that little house of yours. *(CB pulls Matt away by the arm.)*

CB. Matt, dude, chill. There's nothing wrong with him being here. We're having a good time.

MATT. We WERE until he walked in.

CB. Leave him alone, man. Let him stay.

MARCY. CB! My parents would kill me if they knew there was a homosexual in our house!

CB. Marcy, there are seven people upstairs on Ecstasy fucking in your parents' bed! Relax! *(Tricia, who is BEYOND trashed, walks over to Beethoven and falls against him.)*

TRICIA. Did you hear there's a homosexual in the house? *(She falls down, spilling her beer all over Beethoven. Marcy runs over to her and begins fanning her, freaked out.)*

MATT. See! Look! Now that he's here, people are starting to die.

BEETHOVEN. I'm leaving. Prick. *(Beethoven throws his cup down and Matt lunges at him. CB is able to grab him and keep him away.)*

CB. *(To Beethoven.)* No! Don't go. *(To Matt.)* Matt, calm down. Go inside and get a beer or something.

MATT. I'm not going anywhere until this little faggot has walked his faggoty ass out of here!

CB. He's not going anywhere.

BEETHOVEN. *(Angry.)* CB, shut up, I'm leaving.

CB. No!

MATT. Yeah, isn't your dad waiting for you? *(CB grabs Matt's arm and twists it behind his back. Matt screams in pain. The gang gasps.)* What the fuck are you doing, man?

CB. Apologize to him. Right now.

MATT. Fuck no! *(CB twists his arm further. Another scream.)*

MARCY. Let him go, CB!

VAN. Dude, turn him loose. He's your friend.

CB. *(Pointing to Beethoven.)* So is Beethoven. *(He pushes Matt to the ground. They all run over from [the still passed out] Tricia to Matt.)*

MATT. *(To CB.)* I'm gonna kill you. *(CB stands beside Beethoven.)*

CB. You guys make me sick. *(To Beethoven.)* Are you okay?

BEETHOVEN. *(In shock.)* Yeah.

CB. Good. *(He grabs him and kisses him AGAIN in front of everyone. They all gasp, REALLY loud this time. Everything is still. CB's sister drops her drink.)*

CB'S SISTER. *(Mortified.)* Oh my God.

VAN. *(Laughing.)* Oh my God.
MARCY. *(Disgusted.)* Oh my God!
MATT. *(In total shock.)* Oh my God. *(Tricia comes to and says:)*
TRICIA. Oh my God, y'all, I think I'm gonna puke.
ALL. *(Except CB and Tricia.)* Me too.
BEETHOVEN. *(Scared, to CB.)* What did you just do?
CB. I think we need to get out of here now. *(They run offstage. Lights out.)*

"NOCTURNE"

Lights up on Beethoven and CB.

BEETHOVEN. That was a very stupid thing you did.
CB. Was it?
BEETHOVEN. You realize we can't go back to school now, don't you? Well, you can, but I can't.
CB. Where do you want to go? I have a car. We can leave tonight. I'm game. Let's go.
BEETHOVEN. Are you on crack? I'm not running away with you! I never want to see you again as long as I live! In fact, I think that I HATE YOU! *(Beat.)* What did you think that would accomplish?! Did you not stop to think about what it would mean for me?
CB. Are you sorry that I did it?
BEETHOVEN. YES!
CB. That I kissed you or that I kissed you in front of them?
BEETHOVEN. BOTH!
CB. Then I'm sorry. I thought that you wanted me to.
BEETHOVEN. Well, that's mighty presumptuous of you. *(Pulling a CD from his pocket.)* Here. I made you this mix. It's all the Chopin you could ever want. I'm kind of, like, going through this Chopin phase. This is all so weird.
CB. Look, I'll tell them all that it was me just trying to prove a point.
BEETHOVEN. What point would that be?!
CB. I don't know. That it's okay to be different.
BEETHOVEN. And you needed me as a visual aid?!

28

CB. I can fix things.
BEETHOVEN. I don't think you can.
CB. I was sticking up for you! That's what you said you wanted!
BEETHOVEN. Sticking up for me is one thing! Sticking your tongue in my mouth in front of everybody is quite another! I can't believe you've done this to me! What am I going to do?
CB. You could kiss me. *(Without missing a beat ...)*
BEETHOVEN. Okay. *(Beethoven throws himself onto CB and they kiss. Lights out.)*

"THE HANGOVER"

> *The sound of a rooster crowing. Lights up on Tricia, Marcy and Matt, sitting on the ground. Matt is shirtless. Tricia's wearing sunglasses and is probably still very intoxicated. Marcy is staring dreamily at Matt. She sings. The following is delivered slowly, except for Marcy who has an overabundant amount of energy.*

MATT. Did that really happen last night or did I dream it?
MARCY. No. We definitely had a threesome. Well, Tricia passed out pretty early on.
MATT. No, I meant the part about CB kissing that ... thing last night.
MARCY. That happened too.
TRICIA. Do you guys have to scream? Shit. Talk at a normal volume. *(They weren't screaming.)*
MARCY. Sorry, sweetie.
MATT. That's fucked up. We shower together after practice. What if he rapes me or something?
MARCY. That is fucked up, but I had a really good time with you though.
MATT. I mean, CB! Come on! Who knew?
MARCY. Matt, have you thought about who you're taking to the prom?
TRICIA. *(Incredulous.)* Don't.
MATT. Do you think they have sex and shit?

29

MARCY. I was thinking maybe we could go see a movie tonight or something?

TRICIA. Does anyone have a cigarette?

MARCY. Do you remember how you told me you loved me last night? Did you mean it?

MATT. It doesn't make sense.

TRICIA. I want yogurt.

MARCY. Hey Matt! Why don't you and I go get in the hot tub while Tricia goes to the store and gets yogurt?!

MATT. What if he thinks about me when he jerks off?

TRICIA. I don't want to go anywhere.

MARCY. Sure you do! *(She stands up and starts to drag Tricia up.)*

TRICIA. Let go of me, freak!

MATT. This is all that little faggot's fault. I don't know what he did to CB, but I'm gonna fucking kill him. I'm gonna fucking —

MARCY. Are you crying?

MATT. No. The sun's in my eyes.

TRICIA. I don't feel good. *(Matt runs offstage and vomits. Marcy picks up the bottle of Malibu rum and downs it.)*

MARCY. Do you think he's into me?

TRICIA. Honestly?

MARCY. Since when are we honest with each other?

TRICIA. Oh. Yeah. Right. He's TOTALLY into you! *(Lights out.)*

"FIRE IS BAD"

Lights up on what looks like a booth. There is a chair facing it. Behind it sits Van's sister. There's a sign at the corner of the booth that says: THE DOCTOR IS IN. CB enters and Van's sister smiles.

VAN'S SISTER. Well, it's about mutherfucking time!

CB. Well, if a certain someone would stop getting thrown into solitary, then another certain someone could come visit more often.

VAN'S SISTER. *(Warmly.)* Sit down! Sit down!

CB. *(Reading the sign.)* "The Doctor Is In."

VAN'S SISTER. Boy, is she ever.

CB. Very funny.

VAN'S SISTER. I thought you might like it. How have you been?! How is everybody?!

CB. Everybody's pretty much the same. How are you?

VAN'S SISTER. I'm great. I'm doing really well. I've taken up knitting. I know that sounds cheesy, but it's been really good for me and I made you something! *(She holds up a scarf, but it's not nearly as interesting as the handcuffs that are restraining her hands.)*

CB. It's beautiful! Wow! Thanks. I'll wear it often. Don't the handcuffs seems a little unnecessary?

VAN'S SISTER. Are you kidding? I love them! They're kinky and you know me ...

CB. I do.

VAN'S SISTER. *(Mockingly authoritative.)* Besides, it's for your protection.

CB. I'm not scared.

VAN'S SISTER. *(Grinning.)* Maybe you should be.

CB. When are you getting out of here already?

VAN'S SISTER. As soon as I can say three simple words: "Fire is bad." But I'm not in any hurry to rush out of here. They've got me on great drugs! Can I just say: I LOVE LITHIUM! You've gotta try it!

CB. Don't say shit like that. There are people who miss you out there.

VAN'S SISTER. Those people out there are just as crazy as the ones in here. *(She thinks on this.)* Did that sound cliché?

CB. Maybe not as much as "I love lithium."

VAN'S SISTER. I miss you!!! I think you should burn something down and you can join me here! We would have so much fun!

CB. Ugh! Fire. Is. Bad!

VAN'S SISTER. Ha ha. So, what's going on in your life?

CB. *(Blasé.)* Not much. I'm failing like three classes. I kissed Beethoven. And my sister's decided she's Wiccan this week. But that's just this week, I mean, she's gone completely —

VAN'S SISTER. WHAT?

CB. Wiccan. It's some sort of spooky goth thing. I don't really get it.

VAN'S SISTER. You kissed WHO?

CB. It wasn't a big deal. I kissed him last night at a party. In front of everybody. Although, it wasn't the first time.

VAN'S SISTER. Waitwaitwait. Slow down. Beethoven?! Skinny, dorky Beethoven that we all make fun of?

CB. Yeah, the same one you were in love with.

VAN'S SISTER. When I was eight! This is a joke, right? My brother put you up to this, didn't he?

CB. Nope. True story.

VAN'S SISTER. Was it, like, a dare or something?

CB. No.

VAN'S SISTER. You just kissed him? Out of nowhere?

CB. Sort of.

VAN'S SISTER. And you're okay with this?

CB. I think so.

VAN'S SISTER. So?

CB. So?

VAN'S SISTER. So, what does this mean?

CB. I don't know.

VAN'S SISTER. Did you enjoy it?

CB. I wanted to do it.

VAN'S SISTER. Why?

CB. Because I felt like it.

VAN'S SISTER. Major parts of this story are missing, CB. What HAPPENED?

CB. Well, the first time we were in the music room.

VAN'S SISTER. At school?!

CB. Yeah, and we were talking. Actually we were fighting and then we were talking and I just kissed him.

VAN'S SISTER. And the second time?

CB. Party at Marcy's house.

VAN'S SISTER. And people saw?

CB. I wanted them to.

VAN'S SISTER. Oh my God. I don't believe this.

CB. Is it so hard to believe?

VAN'S SISTER. Yes!

CB. Why?

VAN'S SISTER. Because you did something different! You've always been so … predictable.

CB. Oh great. Here we go.

VAN'S SISTER. It's true! You know it's true. Kissing Beethoven is something that's so completely out of character for you. I mean, for a straight guy to kiss a gay guy — that's, like, something. That's … HOT!

CB. What if I'm not straight?

VAN'S SISTER. Are you coming out of the closet?

CB. I didn't say that.

VAN'S SISTER. But you didn't not say it either.

CB. Not not saying something isn't the same as saying something.

VAN'S SISTER. No offense, CB, but I don't think you're cool enough to be gay. Don't get me wrong, I love you to death, but if I had to imagine you giving a shit about home decoration or musical theatre, I just don't see it.

CB. Now you're using stereotypes.

VAN'S SISTER. Sorry, Miss Manners, but I'm in a bit of a shock right now.

CB. We had sex, too.

VAN'S SISTER. Ex-fucking-scuse me!?

CB. Yeah. After the party. We left and we had sex.

VAN'S SISTER. HOLY FUCKING SHIT!!! YOU'RE A HOMO, CB!!!

CB. Just because I did something that I wanted to do doesn't make me a homo. I've smoked pot. Doesn't mean I'm a pothead. I've drank plenty of beer. Doesn't make me a drunk. You set that little redheaded girl's hair on fire. Doesn't make you a pyromaniac.

VAN'S SISTER. *(Correcting him.)* Well, actually, technically it does.

CB. Okay. Bad example.

VAN'S SISTER. Are you going to do it again?

CB. I don't know. Maybe.

VAN'S SISTER. Do you have feelings for him?

CB. I don't know. I've grown up questioning everything I do. When we were kids, everybody — mostly YOU — told me what I was doing was wrong. It made me so self-conscious about everything. Good grief! It takes me an hour to get dressed every morning! I'm always thinking about what people are going to say or what they're going to think. And when I kissed him, I didn't care or wonder what anyone was going to think, I just did it.

VAN'S SISTER. That wasn't an answer. *(A silence passes.)*

CB. I can't stop thinking about him.

VAN'S SISTER. It sounds like love to me.

CB. What do I do?

VAN'S SISTER. You have to tell him.

CB. I can't.

VAN'S SISTER. Then resign yourself to being alone for eternity. That'll be five cents, please.

CB. I love it when we play doctor. *(She laughs.)*

VAN'S SISTER. *(Smiling.)* So, I guess this means we're not getting back together when I get out.

CB. Oh, so now you wanna get out of here, huh?

VAN'S SISTER. Fuck yeah! I didn't realize what I was missing! *(Beat.)* Oh, by the way. My brother told me about your dog. I'm really sorry. *(He had forgotten all about that.)*

CB. Oh. Yeah. Thanks.

VAN'S SISTER. It's a shame I'm locked up in here. We could've cremated him. *(He stares at her unimpressed.)* Sorry. Bad joke. *(A silence.)*

CB. Hey, why'd you do it?

VAN'S SISTER. What? Burn the bitch's hair off? Torch her tresses? Light her locks?

CB. Tell me.

VAN'S SISTER. Her hair is a symbol of innocence and my lighter is a symbol of corruption. God told me to do it. The devil made me do it. Charles Manson is just so damn persuasive. She is Joan of Arc and I am the townspeople of Salem. I did it for Jodie Foster! Boredom — plain and simple. It was a political statement! Allegorical! Metaphorical! A cry for help. A plea of insanity. *(Flexing her forefinger.)* Redrum! Redrum!

CB. Be serious!

VAN'S SISTER. Can't we just blame the government or the educational system? Puberty? P.M.S.? My parents?

CB. No.

VAN'S SISTER. Fine then. I did it because I felt like it.

CB. That's no excuse.

VAN'S SISTER. Really? You used it no less than five minutes ago.

CB. Public displays of affection and random acts of violence are two different things.

VAN'S SISTER. Are they? *(Beat.)* They say that love and hate are the closest two emotions.

CB. I'll bite. Why do you hate the little redheaded girl?

VAN'S SISTER. Because you used to love her.

CB. You did it because of me?

VAN'S SISTER. Yes. I just love you so intensely that it borderlines psychotic. You're all I ever think of.

CB. Seriously?

VAN'S SISTER. Nah, I'm just fucking with you. It's the lithium talking.

CB. *(Starting to stand.)* I'm gonna go now.

VAN'S SISTER. Wait! Don't! I was pregnant.

CB. Why can't you be honest with me like I've been with you?

VAN'S SISTER. I am. I was pregnant. *(Beat.)* Don't worry. It wasn't yours. I had just gotten an abortion the day before and the next day in Biology, we were ironically learning about reproduction. I'm listening to Miss Rainey talking about fallopian tubes, the uterus, eggs and I'm feeling sick to my stomach already. Trying to zone out on anything I can. So I start reading a note over Miss Puritanical Princess' shoulder and she's telling her friend *(Aping perfection.)* "how happy she is that she's a virgin and that she's going to stay that way until she gets married and how repulsed she is by all of the whores at our school." Without thinking, I reached into my pocket for my cute, little red Bic lighter and lit her cute, little red hair on fire. And every day in therapy, they ask me if I'm sorry yet and I just can't be. No matter how hard I try. Bitches like that make me sick. They've made me sick. I am officially sick, psychotic, unrepentant and unremorseful. I've been branded a sociopath and I have no choice but to believe it. *(CB smiles at her.)*

CB. Pregnant?

VAN'S SISTER. Pregnant.

CB. You're fucking with me again? *(She smiles. She pushes a button on her wrists and the cuffs fall off. She tosses the toy handcuffs aside. A buzz is heard.)* I gotta go. Visiting time is over.

VAN'S SISTER. I'm glad you came.

CB. Yeah, me too.

VAN'S SISTER. Before you go — I guess I don't have to ask how everyone reacted.

CB. To your incarceration?

VAN'S SISTER. I meant the kiss.

CB. Are you kidding? We hightailed it out of there so fast, I didn't even have time to look.

VAN'S SISTER. Smart kid.

CB. Although, I think my sister mouthed "I hope you die" at me across the breakfast table this morning. But the clock is ticking and I guess I'll find out how everybody else votes tomorrow at school.

VAN'S SISTER. Good luck.

CB. Thanks.

VAN'S SISTER. CB, I'm so proud of you for breaking through. For setting one foot outside the norm and giving no apologies. Promise me that you won't apologize.

CB. I won't.

VAN'S SISTER. I have faith in you. *(They embrace.)* And next

time when you come, if you could just maybe stick a book of matches up your ass, I'd be your best friend forever. *(CB gets up and leaves, but not before saying —)*
CB. *(Smiling.)* You already are. *(Lights out. In darkness —)*
VAN'S SISTER. Hey, Blockhead! You forgot your scarf! *(The sound of a cell door closing.)*

"OUR SISTER OF MERCY"

Lights up on CB's sister, who is crying. Van walks in and sees her. He sits down beside her.

VAN. What's wrong?
CB'S SISTER. I hate him.
VAN. Who?
CB'S SISTER. My brother, you moron!
VAN. Because he's gay?
CB'S SISTER. I can't believe this! Everybody's treating me like a leper because I'm forced to share the same house as him. We share the same bathroom! What if I get some … some … gay disease?
VAN. That would suck. But come on. You're smarter than that. What is this really about?
CB'S SISTER. He knows how I feel about Beethoven!
VAN. Have you voiced your concerns to him?
CB'S SISTER. I don't want to talk to him!
VAN. You wanna smoke? *(He pulls out a pipe.)*
CB'S SISTER. I guess. I've never done it before. How do I do it? *(He shows her the pipe.)*
VAN. Here. I'll teach you. This is the carb. Put your finger over it. Just hold, suck, let go of the carb and continue sucking. *(She does this as he lights it for her. She breathes in and keeps it in like a pro.)*
CB'S SISTER. I've never smoked pot before. *(She exhales with ease.)*
VAN. I smoked my blanket.
CB'S SISTER. *(Ignoring that comment.)* It's not fair! Why does he have to be my brother?
VAN. Maybe it's because you have the same parents. Or something.
CB'S SISTER. Do you think I should tell my parents? Maybe if I

did, they'd send him away.

VAN. They should send him to Amsterdam. I think a lot of homos go to Amsterdam. I wanna go to Amsterdam. Not because I'm a homo. You can smoke everywhere in Amsterdam. I definitely wanna go to Amsterdam.

CB'S SISTER. You're retarded.

VAN. *(Smiling and nodding.)* Perhaps I am. *(Beat.)* Hey, you know what would be the perfect revenge? If you had sex with your brother's best friend. *(Putting his arm around her.)* Guys really hate that.

CB'S SISTER. Ewww. I'm not losing my virginity to you.

VAN. Well, I think he'd be equally upset by you giving his best friend a blowjob.

CB'S SISTER. I guess. I've never done it before. How do I do it?

VAN. Here. I'll teach you. *(Lights out.)*

"SALISBURY STEAK"

Lights up on Marcy, Tricia, Van and Matt eating lunch in the cafeteria. They are eating in silence.

MARCY. I hate Salisbury steak. *(No response.)* Hey, don't you guys hate the obligatory scene in teen movies where someone describes all of the inhabitants of each table? You know, like, how they say, "The stoners sit there. The cool kids sit there. The geeks sit there. The jocks sit there. Blah blah blah." It's in every movie! Don't you guys hate that? *(Again, no response.)*

TRICIA. I think we're all dodging a certain topic here. One that perhaps needs to be addressed. I mean, we can talk about this like adults, right? I know I'm not the only one with an opinion. And he is our friend. So, all I'm saying is that — *(New tactic.)* Oh Jesus Christ! WILL SOMEONE JUST FUCKING SAY SOMETHING ALREADY?!

VAN. About what?

MARCY. CB, dumbass.

VAN. Oh. I saw him in the halls. I like the shirt he's wearing. *(Matt sits and seethes. The girls look at Van like he's insane.)*

MARCY. Well, the Bible says that homosexuality is a sin. I think.

TRICIA. Good. This is good. I'll go next. I'm A-OK with being gay! But with that said, I think it's really gross to see two guys kiss. Or to hold hands. *(Big confession.)* Drag queens frighten me. *(She gets lost in thought. Snapping back:)* Would anyone else like to share? *(Silence.)* Guys? *(Silence.)* Anyone? *(They all look at her like she's nuts. She's embarrassed.)* I mean, yeah, I hate Salisbury steak, too.

VAN. Dude, you know what's even worse than Salisbury steak? Mexican pizza! I fuckin' hate Mexican pizza! It's like, they didn't invent it, so why do they swoop into high-school cafeterias and try to take credit for it? If I want Mexican food, I'll go get a taco! Not a pizza! It just doesn't make sense, right? It's like — I dunno, like — Australian spaghetti — or some shit like that. It just doesn't make sense. Fuck, man. Why don't we ever have tacos? Or like Burrito Day? If I was class president, I'd insist on Burrito Day. Not this Mexican pizza shit. But you know what else is good? Hamburgers. Even in a high-school cafeteria, a hamburger's always nice. You sort of can't go wrong with it. Sure the meat's always a little tough and the bun's always a little hard, but I can eat a hamburger, yo. But only if it's — *(Matt, so pissed he can no longer contain it, slams his fist against the table. They all look at him, shocked.)*

MATT. *(Through clenched teeth.)* It's not right.

VAN. See! He understands! There's no such thing as Mexican pizza!

TRICIA. *(Condescendingly.)* Sweetie, I think he's talking about CB.

VAN. Oh.

MARCY. Well, the Bible says —

MATT. I don't give a shit about what the Bible says! It's just fucking wrong! It's disgusting and it's just — it's just WRONG! And I fucking hate that kid for fucking with my best friend's head! *(He looks like he might cry out of anger and frustration.)*

TRICIA. What are you going to do?

MATT. I'm not going to stand by as my best friend becomes a — *(He can't say it.)* you know!

TRICIA. Maybe you should have a talk with Beethoven.

MATT. Maybe I should beat his fucking face in.

TRICIA. Violence never solves anything. *(Thinking about this.)* Okay, I'm wrong. Actually it does. But for the sake of your friendship with CB, perhaps you should have a civilized conversation with Beethoven. Something along the lines of, "It really hurts me that you're pursuing a sexual relationship with my friend."

VAN. Tricia's right. Just tell him that —

MARCY. *(Excited.)* Oooh! Oooh! Tell him that the Bible says it's wrong!

VAN. No, tell him that CB is, like, dead or something! We could all pretend like he's dead, but he's not really, but Beethoven will think that he is and then he'll stop liking him! And then we'll tell CB that Beethoven is dead! And then they'll both think that the other is dead! It's genius! I'm a fucking genius. *(Matt stands up and leaves, his fists clenching. A silence.)*

MARCY. He seems really pissed. Do you think one of us should go after him?

TRICIA. Nah. I find it's best not to interfere with feuding lovers.

VAN. Are Beethoven and CB feuding?

TRICIA. I meant Matt and CB, ding dong.

MARCY. Wait. What?

TRICIA. Oh my God. You guys are so blind! Matt's in love with CB. That's what this is all about. It doesn't take Nancy Drew to solve that case. I figured it out and I'm the stupid one.

VAN. I don't buy it. *(CB's sister enters and heads towards their table.)*

TRICIA. The only thing you buy comes in a baggie from a guy who calls himself "The Doober."

VAN. Blow me. *(Thinking he's talking to her, CB's sister runs away in shame.)*

TRICIA. Repressed homosexual anger isn't all that uncommon. Think about it. He's always, like, faggot this and faggot that. He's totally obsessed with CB and totally jealous of Beethoven. *(Beat.)* Here. Let me give you an example: Take fucking-fatty-fat-fucking-fatass-Frieda I think we can all agree that she's the biggest carpet-muncher who's ever walked the face of the fucking earth, correct?

VAN. She's totally in love with Craig Kovelsky!

TRICIA. Well, uh, well, she's a ginormous fucking heifer of a blimp.

VAN. Frieda weighs like eighty pounds!

TRICIA. Shut up, Van. Now, don't you think she's jealous of us because we're pretty and I'm popular? So much so that she probably OBSESSES about how much she hates us all day long?

VAN. She never talks about you. But you always talk about her! *(Figuring it out.)* It's you that's obsessed with her!

TRICIA. Oh no no no, my little stoned friend. You've missed the turn and are heading towards a dead end.

VAN. No no no no no no no — move over, Nancy Drew! Scooby Doo's drivin' this van! *(Another genius idea.)* So, following the logic you so graciously presented us with — repressed homosexuality rears its ugly head in the form of obsession and jealousy so, holy shit! *(Gasp.)* Do you know what this means?

TRICIA and MARCY. WE'RE NOT LESBIANS!! *(Tricia and Van look at Marcy, strangely, who looks away holding a spoonful of Jello.)*

MARCY. At least I'm not.

TRICIA. What's that supposed to mean, you TWAT?

MARCY. Oh nothing. I just think it's really strange how you never used to invite me to your sleepovers with her in eighth grade.

TRICIA. That's because you make weird sex sounds when you sleep!

MARCY. I DO NOT! *(To Van.)* I do not. *(To herself.)* I do not.

TRICIA. You're both assholes! I'm not jealous of Frieda and I'm not in love with her either! She and Craig Kovelsky can have each other! I hope he gets lost in her FAT ROLLS! *(She grabs her bag and huffs off.)*

MARCY. TRISH!!!

TRICIA. *(Icily.)* Don't. *(They eat their lunch in silence.)*

MARCY. *(A troubling thought …)* This is the cool table, right? *(The lights fade out, as they continue to eat their lunch.)*

"WARSAW WAR SONG"

Lights up on CB, who addresses the audience — continuing his letter. The angry runs of "Revolutionary Etude" are heard.

CB. *(Excited, almost giddy.)* I read that Chopin was on his way to Paris when he heard of the fall of his city, Warsaw, to the Russians. He locked himself in a room and composed his "Etude in C Minor: Opus 10, Number 12," or the "Revolutionary Etude," in response. *(Beat.)* Don't you see how perfect it was? Me and Beethoven would be revolutionaries! With our sporks raised, we would charge through this high school showing everyone how to be themselves and no one would have to apologize. *(He listens to Beethoven.)*

"MAL DI LUNA"

Lights up on Beethoven at the piano. He is playing "Revolutionary Etude" by Chopin. CB approaches with a brown paper sack. He starts unpacking lunch on the piano.

CB. I brought you lunch. *(Beethoven stops. He gives CB a look of despair and frustration.)* Hey, we made it halfway through the day and I only got called a queer three times.

BEETHOVEN. That's because people are scared you'll beat them up.

CB. Don't worry. I've already started spreading the word that if they mess with my boyfriend, I'll be kicking some ass. *(He kisses the top of Beethoven's head.)*

BEETHOVEN. Your boyfriend?

CB. Well, I thought the other night sort of sealed the deal.

BEETHOVEN. Slow down, CB.

CB. Why?

BEETHOVEN. Because I don't want a boyfriend.

CB. Nonsense!

BEETHOVEN. We shared a moment.

CB. *(Laughing.)* We shared more than that.

BEETHOVEN. This can't happen.

CB. What can't?

BEETHOVEN. We can't just start a relationship. I mean, you've gotta be a little more realistic.

CB. Give people time. They'll get used to the idea.

BEETHOVEN. How can I expect "people" to get used to the idea when I'm not used to the idea!

CB. *(With a goofy grin.)* I'm falling in love with you. *(Beethoven can't help but blush. He snaps back to reality.)*

BEETHOVEN. This is retarded. *(CB picks up a carton of yogurt from the piano.)*

CB. Do you like yogurt?

BEETHOVEN. No.

CB. Shit. Neither do I. I was hoping you'd want it. *(Holding up two sandwiches.)* Ham or bologna?

BEETHOVEN. CB, I really need to practice.

CB. You really need to eat.

BEETHOVEN. *(To himself.)* I'm in the fucking "Twilight Zone."

CB. Ham it is.

BEETHOVEN. *(Losing it.)* CB! Just stop! Okay? This isn't what I want.

CB. What's the problem?

BEETHOVEN. THIS is the problem! I'm a little stressed out right now and I'm trying to calm my nerves by playing the piano and you're turning into Donna Reed before my very eyes.

CB. Who?

BEETHOVEN. Never mind. Look. The other night was great, but let's just call it one of those things. You go back to being yourself and I'll even let you hit me now and then for old time's sake. This is just too weird.

CB. Remember the other day when I asked you if you were gay and you said you didn't know? You'd never been with a man before? Well, now you have, so what's the verdict?

BEETHOVEN. *(Beaten.)* I don't know. I'm trying not to think about the other night. *(CB sits down next to him and begins kissing his neck.)*

CB. I can't think of anything else. *(Beethoven squirms away. CB gets up. Now he's getting perturbed.)* Fine. I'll leave you alone.

BEETHOVEN. Thank you.

CB. But eat something. You're too skinny.

BEETHOVEN. Fine. *(CB grabs his backpack and starts to exit. He turns around and looks at Beethoven.)* Just give me time.

CB. Yeah. *(He leaves. Once the coast is clear, Beethoven smiles.)*

BEETHOVEN. *(To himself.)* Oh my God. *(He resumes his playing and he can't get the grin off of his face. Several moments pass. Matt enters, unseen by Beethoven.)*

MATT. Hey there, Liberace. *(Beethoven stops playing and turns around. He tries hard to conceal the fact that he's terrified ...)*

BEETHOVEN. You're not supposed to be in here.

MATT. Where's your boyfriend?

BEETHOVEN. He's not my boyfriend. I didn't have anything to do with what happened the other night.

MATT. You sort of did.

BEETHOVEN. Just leave me alone, okay? Please. I didn't do anything.

MATT. Play something. *(Beethoven doesn't move. Matt takes his fin-*

ger and bends it backwards, leading him to the keys. Beethoven begins to play "Moonlight Sonata." Matt becomes transfixed by the music.) So, are you two, like, a couple now? Are you going to parade around the halls holding hands? Go to prom together? *(Beat.)* Did you have sex with him? *(Beethoven doesn't answer, prompting Matt to slam his head down on the keys.)* Keep playing. *(Matt climbs atop the piano.)* Can't you people just keep it hidden? Instead of throwing it in our faces? *(Beethoven stops and looks at him. It's in this moment that he realizes Matt's secret. Matt jumps down from the piano.)* CB is not like you. And if you so much as look at him again, I'll kill you. You got that, perv? *(Beethoven stops playing. Matt starts to exit.)*

BEETHOVEN. No.

MATT. What? *(Matt goes back to the piano.)* What did you just say?

BEETHOVEN. I said no. Pigpen. *(Matt puts his hand in front of Beethoven's mouth and quickly slams the piano lid down on his hand. He slams the lid down on his hands again. Beethoven screams in Matt's hand.)*

"TAPHEPHOBIA"

Lights up on CB, who addresses the audience — continuing his letter.

CB. Frederic Chopin died of tuberculosis on October 17, 1849. He had two requests upon dying. He was terrified of being buried alive, so he asked that his heart be removed from his body. It was. It's entombed in a pillar in the Church of the Holy Cross in Warsaw. The second request was that Mozart's "Requiem" be sung at his funeral. The piece requires female voices, but the Church of the Madeleine didn't let women sing in their choir. They delayed the service for two weeks while the powers that be argued. In the end, they honored his final wish. *(Long beat.)* Beethoven didn't leave a note. So, I don't know if he had any last requests. *(A school bell rings.)*

"PEER COUNSELING"

Classroom. CB takes his seat where CB's sister, Marcy, Tricia and Van are seated. CB is miserable. He does not want to be there. Marcy is blubbering into a Kleenex. CB's sister is wearing, for the first time, what would be considered normal attire, despite the fact that it's black. The teacher, whose voice is the "woh-wohs" of a trombone, asks a question. In response —

TRICIA. I'll go first. Beethoven was very talented. I definitely connected with him on that level. His suicide was an enormous shock to me, anyway. I mean, like, I never thought he would do something like that in a million years. *(She thinks.)* That's all. *(The trombone sounds again.)*

VAN. What do I think about it? Well, I mean, if I had to go, I would definitely want it to be of an overdose. What kind of pills were they anyway?

MARCY. Does it matter? Our good friend is dead! You're being really insensitive. I just wish that he had called me. I would've totally, like, told him everything would be okay and stuff. I don't think he had my number, though. *(The trombone.)*

CB'S SISTER. I think Matt should be put in jail for the rest of his life. Or executed.

MARCY. Why? He didn't kill him.

CB'S SISTER. What Matt did led Beethoven to do what he did!

TRICIA and MARCY. That's hearsay.

CB'S SISTER. And he gets suspended for a week. A slap on the wrist. It's pathetic bullshit. *(The garbled voice screams at her. Sheepishly:)* Sorry. I just don't think it's fair. *(The garbled voice talks, prompting CB to come out of the daze he was in.)*

CB. Huh? *(She asks him the question.)* How does his death make me feel? Stupid. *(They all look at him strangely.)* Oh, come off it! No one even liked him. Who cares? He's dead!

TRICIA. *(Sneering.)* God, that's rude.

CB. That's life, Patty. The world is full of people who have tough lives. But do you see them killing themselves? No. So, he couldn't play the piano anymore. There are people out there who can't walk.

Can't see. Do they give up? No. They keep going. "Pathetic bull-shit," sis? Suicide is pathetic bullshit. It's weak.

CB'S SISTER. Weak? You didn't even go to his funeral! You didn't even say goodbye to him!

CB. *(Losing his shit.)* DID HE SAY GOODBYE TO ME?! I wish he was still here so I could twist his arm behind his back, shove his face in a toilet and tell him that he sucks dick. *(They all begin to berate his insensitivity in unison.)* Can we just stop talking! *(Pleading with them.)* This is exactly what he so selfishly wanted! For us to sit around and pretend like he was still our best friend and sob about how much we'll miss him!

CB'S SISTER. CB. Stop this.

CB. If you miss him so much, why don't you go pray to your witchcraft goddess and ask her to bring him back. Or Matt can dive back into the dirt and dig the "faggot" up and break a few more bones. *(Turning to Van.)* Hey Van! We can get your sister, the pyromaniac, to light him on fire and YOU can roll his ashes into a big, fat joint and y'all can all get high. *(Turning to Marcy and Tricia.)* Marcy, Tricia — here's to "maggot food"! *(To the teacher.)* And then we'll all come back here and we'll talk about how we feel! *(He hits the wall and storms off. There is a long silence. They all stare at the ground. Lights out.)*

"CHANGING EVOLUTION"

Two lights shine on CB and his sister, who stand on opposite sides of the stage. They address the audience.

CB'S SISTER. And when I poked my head out of my cocoon, I realized I had stayed inside for too long. I had, unwittingly, gone from platypus to beaver to walrus to chimpanzee to a human. I had evolved much more than I ever wanted to. Now I would learn to speak and learn to think and ask questions and make friends and lose friends and cry and laugh and maybe fall in love one day and maybe see that love go away and maybe climb a mountain. But I never wanted to do any of these things. Platypuses don't feel things, do they?

CB. The sad thing is that his hands will never heal. That the broken parts of a dead body cannot heal.

CB'S SISTER. Now I'm trapped in this body that will always know regret. A girl who should've been a butterfly, but would still always want to be a platypus.

CB. I hope you're doing well. Sorry for unloading all of this. *(Forcing a smile.)* I bet this is the longest letter you've ever gotten. Thanks for listening. Sincerely. No. Yours truly. Or. Your pen pal. CB. *(The lights change and CB's sister looks to him. The red doghouse appears. It is old and covered with cobwebs, creating a mausoleum-like presence.)*

"BROTHERS AND SISTERS"

CB'S SISTER. Hey.

CB. Hey.

CB'S SISTER. *(Carefully.)* Are you okay?

CB. Why does everyone keep asking me that?! I'm fine! *(CB climbs atop the doghouse. His sister joins him.)*

CB'S SISTER. I know you didn't mean what you said today.

CB. You're wrong. I did.

CB'S SISTER. I know that you loved him.

CB. Look, I went through … something. Some sort of phase. I don't know what it was, but I'm done with it now. Everything's okay. I'm back to normal. This is a good thing.

CB'S SISTER. I don't believe that.

CB. Just stop already, okay? Please. I want to move forward.

CB'S SISTER. I know I was a real bitch about … you two. It stung. That's okay though. In time, I would've been okay with it. I would've been great with it! We're different — you and me. We're special. We're not like them.

CB. I am like them. *(Correction.)* I want to be like them.

CB'S SISTER. That's sad. *(Beat.)* You know, when we were kids, I used to look up to you.

CB. When I was a kid, I was a loser.

CB'S SISTER. No, you weren't. You were great. A little different, but great. Recently, I've seen that quality in you again.

CB. Do you ever feel like you're not a real person? That you're the product of someone's imagination and you can't think for yourself because you're really like just some "creation" and that somewhere there's people laughing every time you fail?

CB'S SISTER. Laugh and the world laughs with you —

CB. Cry and they laugh even harder. *(She kisses him on the cheek and starts to exit.)* Do you think I'm gay?

CB'S SISTER. Maybe. Maybe not. *(Smiling.)* You know, I can't keep up with you. *(Mocking him.)* Find. An. Identity. *(CB laughs.)* Oh, I almost forgot. This came for you. *(She hands him an envelope, then leaves. He looks at it and the wind is knocked out of him.)*

"DEAR CB ... "

The lights dim. CB stands alone in the center of the stage. He is holding in his hand the letter. And just staring at it. He opens it, tentatively. It begins to rain, but just on him. The cast enters and stands in a semi-circle around him.

ALL. Dear CB.

CB'S SISTER. How unexpected to get a letter from you after all these years.

VAN'S SISTER. I thought you had forgotten about me.

VAN. It sounds like you're going through a pretty rough time and having to deal with situations that you feel like you can't handle —

TRICIA. But if anyone is equipped to deal with these things, it's you.

VAN. I promise that things get better.

TRICIA. Hang in there.

TRICIA and VAN. Be strong.

MATT. I'm so sorry for your loss.

MARCY. I was talking to a girl the other day who told me of an incident that happened at her high school.

ALL. There was a boy.

MATT. Bullied.

TRICIA and MARCY. Tormented.

MATT. To the point of opening fire on their cafeteria. He was quiet and awkward. No one ever spoke to him unless it was to insult him. He took the lives of many people. The girl told me that no one ever extended a hand in friendship to this poor child. *(Matt walks to the other side of the stage and stands on his own.)*

ALL. She hadn't.

TRICIA. She said how she wished that she hadn't turned a blind eye to what he was going through.

MARCY. She thinks to herself, how differently things could have been through just one connection. No matter how great or small.

VAN'S SISTER. She lives where I live now. A place where there is no violence. Everyone treats others with kindness, love and respect. If you can imagine such a place, I challenge you to do so. Think on it.

VAN. As for the questions that you are asking yourself and others: Don't concern yourself with death. Immerse yourself in life. Enjoy every moment that you're allowed to but keep asking questions. My dear friend. Don't ever stop asking questions. *(Van crosses to the brick wall and sits on it.)*

MARCY. Also, bear no malice for the ones who leave you.

TRICIA. The only regret they feel now is the regret of not being able to tell you how they really feel.

VAN'S SISTER. They wish that they could say goodbye to the ones they left behind.

MARCY. But sometimes that's not possible.

TRICIA. Even in perfect happiness —

MARCY. Even in nirvana —

TRICIA, MARCY and VAN'S SISTER. They will always have this regret. *(Marcy and Tricia sit on the edge of the stage. Van's sister crosses to the piano and leans on it.)*

CB'S SISTER. A boy recently came to live down the street from me. He's had a tough life, but things are better for him now. He plays the piano like your friend. I often hear his music wafting from an open window, where a small yellow bird sits. Sometimes I cry when I hear it. But mostly I smile. *(CB's sister sits next to Van and puts her head on his shoulder. Beethoven enters. He crosses to CB.)*

BEETHOVEN. He found a dog who likes to sing along. He takes good care of the dog. When we talk, he tells me of a person he knew from where he used to live. Someone very special who means more than anything to him. A person that reminds me of you. *(Beethoven takes his seat at the piano.)*

CB. I apologize for not being there for you before. And I'm not sure that I'll be able to write you again. Just know that there's someone out there thinking about you. Someone who has a vested interest in your success. How I wish I had had the opportunity to meet you. *(Pause.)* Maintain in your heart all that makes you who you are. You are a good man. *(Pause.)* Your Pen Pal. CS. *(As the music reaches the end, he drops the soggy letter and, embracing his own private rain cloud, cries. For his dog. For his friend. For himself.)*

End of Play

PROPERTY LIST

Wooden cross
Cigarettes, lighter
Coffin-shaped purse
Joint
Backpack
Books
Lunch trays with food, milk cartons, utensils
Backpacks with vodka, Kahlua
Bottle of hand sanitizer
Piano
Silk scarf
Cups of beer
Sunglasses
Bottle of Malibu rum
Handcuffs
Knitted scarf
Pipe, lighter
Sack lunch with sandwiches and yogurt
Tissues
Red doghouse
Envelope with letter

SOUND EFFECTS

School bell
Chopin's "Prelude #4 in E Minor, Op. 28/4"
Rooster crowing
Buzz
Cell door closing
Chopin's "Revolutionary Etude"

NEW PLAYS

★ **GUARDIANS by Peter Morris.** In this unflinching look at war, a disgraced American soldier discloses the truth about Abu Ghraib prison, and a clever English journalist reveals how he faked a similar story for the London tabloids. "Compelling, sympathetic and powerful." *–NY Times.* "Sends you into a state of moral turbulence." *–Sunday Times (UK).* "Nothing short of remarkable." *–Village Voice.* [1M, 1W] ISBN: 978-0-8222-2177-7

★ **BLUE DOOR by Tanya Barfield.** Three generations of men (all played by one actor), from slavery through Black Power, challenge Lewis, a tenured professor of mathematics, to embark on a journey combining past and present. "A teasing flare for words." *–Village Voice.* "Unfailingly thought-provoking." *–LA Times.* "The play moves with the speed and logic of a dream." *–Seattle Weekly.* [2M] ISBN: 978-0-8222-2209-5

★ **THE INTELLIGENT DESIGN OF JENNY CHOW by Rolin Jones.** This irreverent "techno-comedy" chronicles one brilliant woman's quest to determine her heritage and face her fears with the help of her astounding creation called Jenny Chow. "Boldly imagined." *–NY Times.* "Fantastical and funny." *–Variety.* "Harvests many laughs and finally a few tears." *–LA Times.* [3M, 3W] ISBN: 978-0-8222-2071-8

★ **SOUVENIR by Stephen Temperley.** Florence Foster Jenkins, a wealthy society eccentric, suffers under the delusion that she is a great coloratura soprano—when in fact the opposite is true. "Hilarious and deeply touching. Incredibly moving and breathtaking." *–NY Daily News.* "A sweet love letter of a play." *–NY Times.* "Wildly funny. Completely charming." *–Star-Ledger.* [1M, 1W] ISBN: 978-0-8222-2157-9

★ **ICE GLEN by Joan Ackermann.** In this touching period comedy, a beautiful poetess dwells in idyllic obscurity on a Berkshire estate with a band of unlikely cohorts. "A beautifully written story of nature and change." *–Talkin' Broadway.* "A lovely play which will leave you with a lot to think about." *–CurtainUp.* "Funny, moving and witty." *–Metroland (Boston).* [4M, 3W] ISBN: 978-0-8222-2175-3

★ **THE LAST DAYS OF JUDAS ISCARIOT by Stephen Adly Guirgis.** Set in a time-bending, darkly comic world between heaven and hell, this play reexamines the plight and fate of the New Testament's most infamous sinner. "An unforced eloquence that finds the poetry in lowdown street talk." *–NY Times.* "A real jaw-dropper." *–Variety.* "An extraordinary play." *–Guardian (UK).* [10M, 5W] ISBN: 978-0-8222-2082-4

DRAMATISTS PLAY SERVICE, INC.
440 Park Avenue South, New York, NY 10016 212-683-8960 Fax 212-213-1539
postmaster@dramatists.com www.dramatists.com

NEW PLAYS

★ **THE GREAT AMERICAN TRAILER PARK MUSICAL music and lyrics by David Nehls, book by Betsy Kelso.** Pippi, a stripper on the run, has just moved into Armadillo Acres, wreaking havoc among the tenants of Florida's most exclusive trailer park. "Adultery, strippers, murderous ex-boyfriends, Costco and the Ice Capades. Undeniable fun." –*NY Post.* "Joyful and unashamedly vulgar." –*The New Yorker.* "Sparkles with treasure." –*New York Sun.* [2M, 5W] ISBN: 978-0-8222-2137-1

★ **MATCH by Stephen Belber.** When a young Seattle couple meet a prominent New York choreographer, they are led on a fraught journey that will change their lives forever. "Uproariously funny, deeply moving, enthralling theatre." –*NY Daily News.* "Prolific laughs and ear-to-ear smiles." –*NY Magazine.* [2M, 1W] ISBN: 978-0-8222-2020-6

★ **MR. MARMALADE by Noah Haidle.** Four-year-old Lucy's imaginary friend, Mr. Marmalade, doesn't have much time for her—not to mention he has a cocaine addiction and a penchant for pornography. "Alternately hilarious and heartbreaking." –*The New Yorker.* "A mature and accomplished play." –*LA Times.* "Scathingly observant comedy." –*Miami Herald.* [4M, 2W] ISBN: 978-0-8222-2142-5

★ **MOONLIGHT AND MAGNOLIAS by Ron Hutchinson.** Three men cloister themselves as they work tirelessly to reshape a screenplay that's just not working—*Gone with the Wind.* "Consumers of vintage Hollywood insider stories will eat up Hutchinson's diverting conjecture." –*Variety.* "A lot of fun." –*NY Post.* "A Hollywood dream-factory farce." –*Chicago Sun-Times.* [3M, 1W] ISBN: 978-0-8222-2084-8

★ **THE LEARNED LADIES OF PARK AVENUE by David Grimm, translated and freely adapted from Molière's *Les Femmes Savantes*.** Dicky wants to marry Betty, but her mother's plan is for Betty to wed a most pompous man. "A brave, brainy and barmy revision." –*Hartford Courant.* "A rare but welcome bird in contemporary theatre." –*New Haven Register.* "Roll over Cole Porter." –*Boston Globe.* [5M, 5W] ISBN: 978-0-8222-2135-7

★ **REGRETS ONLY by Paul Rudnick.** A sparkling comedy of Manhattan manners that explores the latest topics in marriage, friendships and squandered riches. "One of the funniest quip-meisters on the planet." –*NY Times.* "Precious moments of hilarity. Devastatingly accurate political and social satire." –*BackStage.* "Great fun." –*CurtainUp.* [3M, 3W] ISBN: 978-0-8222-2223-1

DRAMATISTS PLAY SERVICE, INC.
440 Park Avenue South, New York, NY 10016   212-683-8960   Fax 212-213-1539
postmaster@dramatists.com   www.dramatists.com

NEW PLAYS

★ **AFTER ASHLEY by Gina Gionfriddo.** A teenager is unwillingly thrust into the national spotlight when a family tragedy becomes talk-show fodder. "A work that virtually any audience would find accessible." *–NY Times.* "Deft characterization and caustic humor." *–NY Sun.* "A smart satirical drama." *–Variety.* [4M, 2W] ISBN: 978-0-8222-2099-2

★ **THE RUBY SUNRISE by Rinne Groff.** Twenty-five years after Ruby struggles to realize her dream of inventing the first television, her daughter faces similar battles of faith as she works to get Ruby's story told on network TV. "Measured and intelligent, optimistic yet clear-eyed." *–NY Magazine.* "Maintains an exciting sense of ingenuity." *–Village Voice.* "Sinuous theatrical flair." *–Broadway.com.* [3M, 4W] ISBN: 978-0-8222-2140-1

★ **MY NAME IS RACHEL CORRIE taken from the writings of Rachel Corrie, edited by Alan Rickman and Katharine Viner.** This solo piece tells the story of Rachel Corrie who was killed in Gaza by an Israeli bulldozer set to demolish a Palestinian home. "Heartbreaking urgency. An invigoratingly detailed portrait of a passionate idealist." *–NY Times.* "Deeply authentically human." *–USA Today.* "A stunning dramatization." *–CurtainUp.* [1W] ISBN: 978-0-8222-2222-4

★ **ALMOST, MAINE by John Cariani.** This charming midwinter night's dream of a play turns romantic clichés on their ear as it chronicles the painfully hilarious amorous adventures (and misadventures) of residents of a remote northern town that doesn't quite exist. "A whimsical approach to the joys and perils of romance." *–NY Times.* "Sweet, poignant and witty." *–NY Daily News.* "Aims for the heart by way of the funny bone." *–Star-Ledger.* [2M, 2W] ISBN: 978-0-8222-2156-2

★ **Mitch Albom's TUESDAYS WITH MORRIE by Jeffrey Hatcher and Mitch Albom, based on the book by Mitch Albom.** The true story of Brandeis University professor Morrie Schwartz and his relationship with his student Mitch Albom. "A touching, life-affirming, deeply emotional drama." *–NY Daily News.* "You'll laugh. You'll cry." *–Variety.* "Moving and powerful." *–NY Post.* [2M] ISBN: 978-0-8222-2188-3

★ **DOG SEES GOD: CONFESSIONS OF A TEENAGE BLOCKHEAD by Bert V. Royal.** An abused pianist and a pyromaniac ex-girlfriend contribute to the teen-angst of America's most hapless kid. "A welcome antidote to the notion that the *Peanuts* gang provides merely American cuteness." *–NY Times.* "Hysterically funny." *–NY Post.* "The *Peanuts* kids have finally come out of their shells." *–Time Out.* [4M, 4W] ISBN: 978-0-8222-2152-4

DRAMATISTS PLAY SERVICE, INC.
440 Park Avenue South, New York, NY 10016 212-683-8960 Fax 212-213-1539
postmaster@dramatists.com www.dramatists.com

NEW PLAYS

★ **RABBIT HOLE by David Lindsay-Abaire.** Winner of the 2007 Pulitzer Prize. Becca and Howie Corbett have everything a couple could want until a life-shattering accident turns their world upside down. "An intensely emotional examination of grief, laced with wit." *–Variety.* "A transcendent and deeply affecting new play." *–Entertainment Weekly.* "Painstakingly beautiful." *–BackStage.* [2M, 3W] ISBN: 978-0-8222-2154-8

★ **DOUBT, A Parable by John Patrick Shanley.** Winner of the 2005 Pulitzer Prize and Tony Award. Sister Aloysius, a Bronx school principal, takes matters into her own hands when she suspects the young Father Flynn of improper relations with one of the male students. "All the elements come invigoratingly together like clockwork." *–Variety.* "Passionate, exquisite, important, engrossing." *–NY Newsday.* [1M, 3W] ISBN: 978-0-8222-2219-4

★ **THE PILLOWMAN by Martin McDonagh.** In an unnamed totalitarian state, an author of horrific children's stories discovers that someone has been making his stories come true. "A blindingly bright black comedy." *–NY Times.* "McDonagh's least forgiving, bravest play." *–Variety.* "Thoroughly startling and genuinely intimidating." *–Chicago Tribune.* [4M, 5 bit parts (2M, 1W, 1 boy, 1 girl)] ISBN: 978-0-8222-2100-5

★ **GREY GARDENS book by Doug Wright, music by Scott Frankel, lyrics by Michael Korie.** The hilarious and heartbreaking story of Big Edie and Little Edie Bouvier Beale, the eccentric aunt and cousin of Jacqueline Kennedy Onassis, once bright names on the social register who became East Hampton's most notorious recluses. "An experience no passionate theatergoer should miss." *–NY Times.* "A unique and unmissable musical." *–Rolling Stone.* [4M, 3W, 2 girls] ISBN: 978-0-8222-2181-4

★ **THE LITTLE DOG LAUGHED by Douglas Carter Beane.** Mitchell Green could make it big as the hot new leading man in Hollywood if Diane, his agent, could just keep him in the closet. "Devastatingly funny." *–NY Times.* "An out-and-out delight." *–NY Daily News.* "Full of wit and wisdom." *–NY Post.* [2M, 2W] ISBN: 978-0-8222-2226-2

★ **SHINING CITY by Conor McPherson.** A guilt-ridden man reaches out to a therapist after seeing the ghost of his recently deceased wife. "Haunting, inspired and glorious." *–NY Times.* "Simply breathtaking and astonishing." *–Time Out.* "A thoughtful, artful, absorbing new drama." *–Star-Ledger.* [3M, 1W] ISBN: 978-0-8222-2187-6

DRAMATISTS PLAY SERVICE, INC.
440 Park Avenue South, New York, NY 10016 212-683-8960 Fax 212-213-1539
postmaster@dramatists.com   www.dramatists.com